James D. Lester, Jr.
Clayton College & State University
Morrow, Georgia

To Accompany
Writing Research Papers:
A Complete Guide
Ninth Edition
by James D.

D1457899

LONG

An imprint of Addison Wesley Longman, Inc.

New York • Reading, Massachusetts • Menlo Park, California • Harlow, England
Don Mills, Ontario • Sydney • Mexico City • Madrid • Amsterdam

Supplements Editor: Donna Campion
Electronic Page Makeup: DTC

Writing Across the Curriculum and Research by James D. Lester and James D. Lester, Jr, to accompany *Writing Research Papers: A Complete Guide,* by James D. Lester, Ninth Edition.

ISBN: 0-321-02761-2

12345678910—CRW—01009998

An Introduction to Research Across the Curriculum

The human species is distinguished by its ability to examine the world systematically and, by that, to create pioneers on the frontiers of the new millennium, such as computer technicians, micro-surgeons, and chemical engineers. What's more, each discipline has different expectations in its methods of inquiry and presentation. Therefore, the research paper assignment becomes an introduction into disciplinary assumptions, procedures, and writing style.

Working within a Discipline

As you begin your research projects, you will have many options in the way you conduct your research. Some disciplines will require you to work in the field, not just the library; therefore, Chapter 2 provides an overview of various methods of inquiry.

You will learn that *social scientists* work from the assumption that human behavior can be observed, tested, and catalogued by observation and experimental testing. Professionals perform thousands of experiments every month. They research stress in the workplace, they study the effects of birth order on the youngest child, or they develop testing mechanisms, such as the SAT test. As a student in the social sciences, you will be asked to perform similar but less exhaustive studies on such topics as the study habits of sixth graders, the typing mannerisms used by students who compose on a computer, or the verbal variations in spontaneous greetings. The world of human behavior awaits these types of investigations.

You will find that *physical scientists* wish to discover, define, and explain the natural world. They operate under the assumption that we can know, and should know, precise data on the flora and fauna, on geological formations, on the various species of animals, and so forth. You may be asked to join a field expedition to catalog one type of fern, to test the water conditions at a local lake, or to locate sinkholes in a confined area.

In contrast, *applied scientists* have a different goal. The applied scientists want to apply the scientific knowledge we possess to make life more efficient, more enduring, and more comfortable. By mathematical formulas and cutting-edge technology they launch spaceships to encircle the globe, find new ways to repair broken bones, and discover new methods of movie animation. You, too, can participate in such experiments by writing a computer program, by investigating systems to control the damage of lightning strikes, or by examining ways to increase the weight of beef cattle.

You will discover that *humanists* in the fine arts, literature, history, and philosophy have a distinctive approach to knowledge. While scientists usually investigate a small piece of data and its meaning, humanists examine an entire work of art (Verdi's opera *Rigoletto*), a period of history (the great depression), or a philosophical theory (existentialism). Rather than use scientific observation, humanists accept a poem or painting as a valid entity and search it subjectively for what it means to human experience.

Designing a Paper

Chapters 2, 3, and 4 of this booklet will explain the *design* of your paper. You will learn the APA style for social science papers, the CBE style for papers in the physical and natural sciences, the number system for papers in the applied sciences and technology, and the footnote style for papers in the humanities.

Suppose, for example, that during one semester you must write three papers for three different professors: a botany research paper, an analysis of Rossini's opera *The Barber of Seville*, and a report on new computer software. The three papers should *not* be similar in form, style, language usage, content, or scholarly assumptions. For the botany paper, you should use the CBE style. For the paper on Rossini, you will need to use the footnote style, and for the computer report you should use the number system. This booklet will help you accomplish that task.

Using the Language of the Discipline

Your use of *specialized language* in your discipline will often mark your paper as an accomplished one because the research paper requires precision in your words and phrases. You must know the language of the discipline. A paper about a painting must use such terms as *symbolism, perspective, design, composition, Pop art, Byzantine art,* and so forth. A paper on nuclear energy, on the other hand, will require such terms as *hydrogen, isotopes,* or *the fissioning of uranium.* The phrasing must be precise without subjective elaboration. Notice the technical language in this next passage:

> The floral composition of the Dickcissel's field consisted of an upper level mainly between three and four feet high, with occasional plants up to five and one-half feet high. This upper level varied widely throughout the field, but it consisted mainly of a fleabane daisy, *Erigeron sp.* There were also concentrations of Queen Anne's Lace, *Daucus Carota,* scattered individuals of goldenrod, *Solidago sp.,* and large individuals of wild lettuce *Lactuca canadensis.*
> —student James C.

This student above writes in technical terminology about the

Dickcissel bird as a naturalist who wants to address other scientists, who will have no trouble understanding the scientific terminology.

If you anticipate, however, that your audience will be general readers without great expertise, write with a general diction. Look now at the more general diction of another student.

> The environment is vital to our lives. We must live by seeing the beauty that nature gives us instead of being blind to the self-destruction. Most people want to protect the earth, but the lack of support and funds make it difficult to change our careless lifestyles. The government has passed a law creating a system of national parks to preserve the land, and the World Bank is ready to provide needed funds to preserve the environment.[2] If the government makes the public aware of the great desire to save the earth, maybe people will help in the struggle to achieve environmental awareness.
>
> —student Kimberly S.

Both James and Kimberly write within themselves for their anticipated audience. James correctly assumes that other scientific minds will examine his work. Kimberly surmises that her language must remain general without the technical precision of the environmental scientist. In part, the language reflects your intellectual sophistication as a writer as well as your perception of the audience.

1 Methods of Inquiry

Methods for investigating a subject overlap from one discipline to another. Your task is to select the one that best suits your purposes as a researcher. Some disciplines within the humanities will require only careful reading and interpretation. Disciplines within the social, physical, and applied sciences, however, may require other techniques, such as tests and measures, field work, and direct observation.

Research requires you to gather evidence and data as you reach for knowledge. Thus, you need to understand several types of evidence. *Accurate evidence* is material based on factual data as developed by you with a questionnaire or as drawn from reliable sources (see "Finding and Reading the Best Sources," pages 83-96 in *Writing Research Papers*). *Relevant evidence* is material that relates to the issue in question, which means your evidence must follow logically from the data. *Representative evidence* means that the data truly represents the constituents or subjects affected by the assertions or findings. For example, evidence on problems with campus parking should come from the students as well as the administration and staff of the campus security force. *Sufficient evidence* means that the data collected is adequate for making judgments. Rather than assert an opinion, such as, "Too many people are running red lights these days," you will need to supply facts based upon careful observation (see pages 11–12): "Three percent of the cars ran stop lights; that may seem like a small percentage, but it

5

represents 62 cars over a period of one week at one intersection."

Research requires you to make an *analysis* of the evidence. For instance, scientific analysis explores the *why* and the *how* of a subject, as well as the *what*. It examines causal relationships and requires you to explain a topic in detail by classifying parts, defining, showing process, comparing, and other techniques. It means that you might need to write a description that explains one of Edison's inventions, write an essay that explains the process of natural selection for one species of insect, or write a detailed definition of chlorine to justify its use in the purification of drinking water. Your analysis of historical events will require similar procedures.

Research also requires you to *interpret* the evidence. This step is the logical one after you have categorized the subject to simplify it for your readers. In other words, you must usually break down the subject with classification and analysis; after that, you must read and interpret the findings. This step requires decision making and/or problem solving.

Rather than merely getting the facts straight, you must now explain or interpret what the facts mean. The kinds of questions you will ask are similar to these:

What does this passage mean?
What does this data tell us?
Can this evidence be applied to other issues or problems?
How can I explain my reading of the problem to others?

Consequently, in making a decision, you will look at a set of alternatives and your preferences. In solving a problem, you will examine it, test your answer or solution, and check the results.

For example, a scientist interprets the collected data to arrive at positive results or negative findings. A radiologist interprets the X-ray to determine the place and severity of a broken bone. A doctor interprets the behavior of a child to reach a diagnosis of Autism. You may be asked to interpret data in one of your science classes. You will certainly confront the task of interpretation in your humanities classes. Writers in philosophy interpret texts on moral, ethical, and legal grounds. Historians examine and interpret the causes for events and their effects on society at the time and on future generations. Writers who examine literature and the fine arts interpret for meanings, themes, and messages as conveyed by a song, a painting, or a story.

However, interpretations in the humanities (e.g. history, philosophy, and art) are not judged *right* or *wrong* or referred to as *positive results* or *negative findings*. They will be judged instead by the readers within the academic community by their marshaling of the evidence, by their imaginative exploration of implications, and by their accordance with reality. Thus, "I Have a Dream," by Martin Luther King, Jr., can be interpreted as a political manifesto, as a historical document, and as an allegorical look at social conditions. The interpretation must cite King's words and must draw support from other published interpretations.

Finally, research in the sciences often requires you to *describe your method.* That is, you must keep a record of the process of research as well as your findings so that you can describe the design of the work, log the procedures, and elaborate on the subjects and the testing apparatus.

The two basic methods of inquiry—theoretical and empirical—are explained below.

Theoretical Inquiry

A theory is an opinion or supposition based on reasoning from known facts. A theory, like a thesis sentence, offers a tentative answer, for example: *allowing some forest fires to burn themselves out is environmentally sound.*

This is the type of theory that your instructor might require you to examine. Only on rare occasions would you be asked to advance your own theory. Thus, your inquiry into a theoretical problem will require four tasks:

1. Address a theoretical problem. Keep in mind that a theory is an assumption, based on accepted principles, that predicts or explains the behavior of humans and the natural environment.

Discovering topics for the theoretical research paper will require you to confront the issues of life—the social, physical, and the psychological aspects. We offer the following list of issues that would demand theoretical examination. You may be asked to explore the implications of such topics within a collaborative study group or on your own. In addition, allow these suggestions to stimulate additional topics worthy of examination in situations that require you to select a topic:

- the theory that phonics is the best method for teaching reading
- the theory that dress codes in schools will reduce violence
- the theory that classrooms provide the best learning environment
- the theory that overpopulation causes stress, violence, and social disorder
- the theory that a college education assures you a better paying job
- the theory that homosexuality is a genetic condition

2. Classify the issues. This task requires you to look carefully and critically at all sides of the problem. What are the alternatives? What aspects have I overlooked? What are issues or questions that my reader might ask? To be successful, then, you will need to categorize the issues within their structural relationships. Sometimes it's fairly simple, such as pro-life and pro-choice, but often the task is more complicated. For example, a classroom provides an ideal learning environment: the students are confined, grouped, well-equipped, and instructed. Yet a field trip offers great benefits: imaginative discovery, unstructured learning, collaboration with peers, among others.

3. Analyze and interpret the literature. As explained above on page 6, research requires you to make an *analysis* of the evidence. What do the experts say about the subject and the issues you have identified? Your research will find the source material, your analysis will sort and identify the relevant data, and your interpretation will explain it for the reader. In many cases you must also trace the background and development of the theory to define, refine, and expand the theoretical ideas. In particular, you must examine the consistency and validity of the theory, which may require you to draw upon the prevailing literature. That is, determine if the experts are consistent in their views and thereby validate the theory.

For example, one student examined the theory behind the practice of mainstreaming children with disabilities in regular classrooms. The task first required careful reading and subsequent citation of the literature, then interviews with two teachers who taught mainstreamed children, and ultimately an analysis and evaluation of both the theory and its practical applications within the classroom environment.

4. Reach a conclusion on its social, psychological, and/or educational ramifications. Your readers will ultimately expect you to provide any conclusions or inferences that you have drawn from the study. Tell us, for example, what you have found about the subject:

> Too often, teachers and administrators opt for classroom work because it's convenient even though evidence shows that field work stimulates the creative elements in a student's education in ways that classroom work cannot.

This writer has reached a conclusion based on the evidence. You must do the same. See pages 23–30 for a theoretical research paper in APA style.

Empirical Inquiry

The word *empirical* means knowledge based on observation or experiment, not on theory. Therefore, a written report that describes original research will be an *empirical study*. It has four primary parts.

1. Introduction. It will introduce your hypothesis, which is something taken to be true for the purpose of investigation and discussion. It is an assumption that must be tested, not merely analyzed. Here's an example:

> Giving high school students in-class instruction on self expression and listening skills will enhance the quality of their interpersonal relationships.

This hypothesis must now be tested in the classroom. That is, you can't merely *discuss* the theory, you must *prove* or *disprove* it.

2. Method. It will explain in detail your methods for proving or disproving the hypothesis—the subjects, the tools, the procedures.

3. Results. It will report the findings of observation, tests, experiments, case studies, investigations, and so forth.

4. Discussion. It will discuss the findings and interpret the implications of your research.

The basis of the study will be your original research, which might take the form of a test, questionnaire, or observation. These are discussed next. Your goal is to gather data that will show the validity of the hypothesis. (See pages 35–43 for an example of one student's proposal for empirical research.)

Techniques for Conducting Research

Field research. You will be required on occasion to go to places outside the classroom, the laboratory, and the library in order to conduct your empirical research. In most cases, you will travel to a special place, such as a field of hybrid corn, a nursing home, a third-grade class at an elementary school, or the site of an archeological dig. You might get lucky and find yourself on a Florida beach in January to examine a species of crab or you might fly to England in April to walk the paths of Dorothy and William Wordsworth in the Lake Country. At other times, you might find yourself in the August heat as you catalogue the ferns at Kentucky's Land Between the Lakes. Another student might conduct an interview of several Native Americans at their reservation casino. Careful record keeping will be necessary, and these notes gathered during field research are called *field writing*.

Observation. Observation takes several forms, including (1) direct observation, (2) tests and measurements, (3) questionnaires, and (4) case histories. You probably can recall taking the ACT or SAT examination, which measured your ability against a broad spectrum of similar candidates to predict your possible success in college. In like manner, you have probably completed questionnaires designed to measure your aptitudes, preferences, and habits. Case studies are used when subjects demand special, in-depth analysis, as with a dyslexic child or a teenager afflicted with anorexia nervosa. Training is a key element with observation of human subjects. Don't use it as the basis for a research paper without supervision and proper training.

1. *Direct observation* can be as simple as counting how many times various vehicles run red lights at a busy intersection. You merely observe, count, and make field notes in your research journal.

2. A *test* is a method for measuring any number of physical or mental conditions. By observing the condition of your blood, a doctor can make a prognosis. By watching you run a 40-yard dash, a coach can determine, in part, the position you might play on the football team. By comparing your test scores with your peers in a classroom, an instructor can determine your ranking within the class. You, too, can conduct a test to prove or disprove a theory. The measurements can then be applied, as shown in the sample research paper on pages 51–55.

3. A *questionnaire* is a scientific instrument designed to measure public response to a set of specific, objective questions. They often produce useful and accurate data that can be tabulated quickly. In general, a random sam-

pling should survey every part of a selected population by such factors as age, sex, race, education, income, residence, and so forth.

In many cases, the student questionnaire is very informal: it is usually a set of questions with yes or no answers distributed to students in a few classes. This type of questionnaire has a low level of reliability. To write a questionnaire that will produce truly reliable data, you must have experience with tests and measurements as well as statistical analysis.

4. A *case study* is a formal report based upon observation and examination of a prearranged subject. For example, it might require the researcher to examine patterns of behavior in order to build a profile of a person as based on biographic data, interviews, tests, and observations over a period of time. Once completed, a case study becomes evidence for a researched report that might be used for psychological counseling, the application of medication, physical therapy, and other programs. Obviously, such work is highly sensitive and governed by regulations on research with human subjects. You should conduct a case study only under the close supervision of your instructor.

Interview. An interview is a formal, prearranged meeting in which you elicit answers on a specific topic. Interviews are an excellent method for gathering information for some types of research papers. Keep in mind criteria for the interview:

Consult with experienced people.
Be courteous and on time for the interview.
Be prepared with a set of questions for initiating the interview.
Be a good listener.
Be flexible in order to originate new questions.

The interview is both collaboration and interaction. You become a participant, so your behavior and questions can affect the outcome. Consequently, try to be as objective as possible.

Finally, it's best if your conclusions are based on several interviews with different knowledgeable people, not just one person. Once you have finished the interviews, weigh and evaluate the opinions as you would with other source material.

A type of interview is the *oral history,* which develops a biographical sketch set against the cultural and social significance of that life in a specific time and place. Its purpose might be psychological, social, medical, or cultural. We often think of oral histories occurring in rural areas, such as Appalachia, but oral histories can occur in an industrial setting (for example, a long-time mechanic at Ford Motor Company), a subculture (for example, a drug dealer who requests anonymity), or a restricted group (for example, a soccer mom, professional golfer, or Harley biker).

Letters. Correspondence provides a written record for research. Ask pointed questions so that correspondents will respond directly to your central issues. As a courtesy, provide a self-addressed, stamped envelope. Questionnaires submitted by mail should include a transmittal letter requesting the favor of a reply. For an example, see *Writing Research Papers,* page 63.

Reading. Critical reading serves most researchers as the primary vehicle for gathering information. Indeed, the library is the soul of any educational institution. To write an interpretation of Hamlet's "madness," you would need to read both the play and secondary sources. To develop a theoretical essay on psychological "denial," you would need to read the essays of professionals. To launch an archeological "dig," you would need to read literature about the site.

The source material should also meet three traditional demands: it must be *recent, representative,* and *sufficient.* That is, use commentary of the last few years, use examples that are typical rather than exotic or rare, and use enough examples to justify your claim (see *Writing Research Papers,* pages 83–95).

In addition, you need to cite facts whenever possible and carefully distinguish the factual data from opinion or inference. A *fact* is documented and proven information. An *inference* is one person's interpretation or conclusion as drawn from specific data. An *opinion* is merely one person's idea unsubstantiated by proof. Use facts in your paper and sometimes inference, but avoid undocumented opinion.

Fact:	Wilson has demonstrated that the average gambler enters a casino with $320.
Inference:	Mackey estimates that the average gambler, who by statistical evidence loses money, has no clue about the odds of winning the various games.
Opinion:	Thompson believes that casino operators find ways to avoid regulations.

In short, you will need to depend heavily upon factual data and the inferences by the experts about the data. Use opinion only when it comes from reputable people in the field. To determine a source's reputation, conduct a citation search (see *Writing Research Papers*, page 86). For more details about evaluating your source material, see "Finding and Reading the Best Sources," pages 83-96 in *Writing Research Papers*.

Making Your Own Inferences

The paper should include your inferences as well, and this is a tough call for some students. Am I merely expressing an opinion or am I drawing inferences from the evidence? A good rule of thumb is this one: Express your ideas in a sentence or two and defend them with citations from primary or secondary source material. That is, if you say something about the lines of a Robert Frost poem, quote the lines for support. If you conclude that life probably exists elsewhere in the universe, support that position by quoting the physicist Carl Sagan or some other authority. If you argue that training in phonics is vital for teaching language to youngsters, support it with documentation.

In your reading, consult *electronic sources* with caution. Use the "edu" and "org" sites that are developed by educational institutions and professional organizations. Be wary of Internet discussion groups, and treat E-mail as "mail," not scholarly matter. (See *Writing Research Papers*, pages 159–60).

Both you and your readers need to know what research has been done on the topic. The *review of the literature* will explain the theoretical framework that ties together the various pieces of research literature. Thereby, it opens the door to your own research, which usually must grow logically and sequentially from previous research. That is, the previous research and your present investigations should be linked incrementally to build the new upon the old. In some instances the review article is a separate, independent work. In other cases, a brief review of the literature will be a part of the introduction to your research paper (see pages 79–80 for an example).

2 The Design of a Paper in the Social Sciences

The social sciences include the fields of psychology, sociology, social work, political science, anthropology, and education. Writers in these disciplines have similar goals and use similar methods for their research and for their reports.

Social scientists work from the assumption that human behavior can be observed, tested, and catalogued, so these researchers, in general, measure and test behavior in both humans and animals. Although most people react to new situations on a whim with an emotional judgment, scientists make methodical and measured judgments. They must abide by rules and specific conventions for testing behavior and interpreting the results. As an apprentice in the social sciences, you will need to learn the conventions of research and then write in an appropriate style. That is, you will find it difficult to share your ideas and findings with others in the social sciences unless you abide by the conventions, no matter how confining and stifling they may seem.

Three methods dominate the field—*theoretical inquiry, observation,* and *experimental testing.* With theoretical inquiry, scientists examine the literature and the issues about the problem. Historical in nature, it requires scientists to trace the literature on the subject and determine the consistency of argument, the validity of theory, and practical applications.

In the observation method, scientists maintain distance from the subject, whereas in the experimental method scientists intercede and intrude upon the subject in some way (see Observation, pages 11–12).

In the experimental method, the social scientist develops a theory or a hypothesis about how or why we behave and then builds a model that will test the theory. The experimental method usually features an experimental group, which researchers stimulate or manipulate in some manner, and a control group, which is identical to the experimental group but without the stimulus. After the experiment, scientists compare what would have happened without intervention (the control group) with what did happen to the experimental group. Along the way, scientists must consider variables in response, the size of the sample, the accurate recording of the data, and above all respect for the subjects being tested.

Ultimately, the social scientist reviews the literature on the subject, reports the findings of this special research, and then interprets and evaluates the results.

Understanding the Writing Style Used in the Social Sciences

Writers in the social sciences prefer the passive voice because it eliminates any hint of bias. The subject, not the actor, receives attention. In the example below, the passive voice eliminates personal intrusion into the discussion, as with "I found evidence that police officers spend" or "I can attribute much of this research to an increased demand."

> Police officers have been shown to spend only 3% of their time in fighting crime (Rupert & Lusk, 1990; Trout, 1991; Gatlin, Marsh, & Warring, 1992). The finding can be attributed to increased demand for accountability within police departments and governmental agencies (see esp. Grober, 1992).

When appropriate, then, step into the background and focus on the subject of the study. That is, separate yourself from the findings and the interpretive discussion. It is considered inappropriate to say: "I believe the findings are relevant to the hypothesis."

However, in your attempt to be objective, do not illogically attribute an action. For example, writing "The researcher observed the subjects over a three-week period" may mislead the reader if the "researcher" refers to you. Use *I* or *we* as the subject, "I observed," or switch to passive voice, "the subjects were observed."

Avoid the word *prove* in discussing your findings because the results are tentative at best until proved *reliable* by replication (that is, other researchers must reach the same conclusions). Use instead such terms as *suggest, show, demonstrate, establish, exhibit,* and *determine:* "the collected data demonstrate" or "the findings suggest."

Use appropriately the present tense to explain *your* findings, to state your conclusions, and to present established knowledge. That is, use the present tense for your generalizations and for your references to stable conditions.

> The findings *suggest* that most police officers spend more time working traffic accidents than investigating crime. In fact, the work load of officers *may encourage* criminals, who usually track carefully the location of specific officers in an area.

However, use the past tense for any condition or activity that took place at a specific time in the past. For example, use the past tense for research completed in the past.

> Thomason and Leftowich (1993) *established* the norm, and Wisner (1994) confirmed it.

Also, use the past tense to set limits on your findings and on the universal claims you might make about the research.

> The subjects, 30 police officers, *exhibited* increased pulse rates.

That statement differs markedly from saying "police officers *exhibit* increased pulse rates," in which the present tense implies that all police offiers always show increased pulse rates. Past tense limits the finding to the specified group in your study. By that, you do not make any claims about all police officers.

Use the past tense for work that you completed during your study.

> In this research, I *attempted* to identify the time available to officers for crime prevention. Thirty police officers *served* as voluntary participants. The subjects *were chosen* at random.

Use the present perfect tense to indicate an activity or condition in the past that began in the past and continues into the present.

> Recent research *has indicated* that police presence *has been sufficient* to deter crime (Berman & Smith, 1994). As a result, some departments *have modified* their deployment of officers and *have begun* using walking patrols, bicycle teams, and highly visible patrol cars.

In addition, take your reader carefully through the study by connecting data and discussion. Do not present a table or figure without discussing it in the text. Avoid any devices of language that call attention to the style of writing rather than the subject. Avoid using metaphor, alliteration, rhyme, and other poetic devices.

Citations in APA Style

See *Writing Research Papers*, Chapter 10, for details about in-text citations, such as this one,

> Jones (1993) determined the time restraints on a select group of police officers.

and for bibliography entries like this,

Menyuk, P., Chesenick, M., Liebergott, J., Korngold, B.,
D'Agostino, R., & Belanger, A. (1991). Predicting
reading problems in at-risk children. <u>Journal of Speech
and Hearing Research, 34,</u> 893-903.

Types of Research Papers in the Social Sciences

Most research papers in the social sciences fall into one of three categories:

> *The Theoretical Paper* is a work that traces the history and applications of a theory.
> *The Report of Empirical Research* is a work that explains the methods and results of your original research.
> *The Review Article* is a work that interprets and sometimes evaluates an article or book.

Each of these is discussed in detail on the following pages.

The Theoretical Paper

A *theoretical paper*, also known as a *thesis paper*, will require you to address the issues surrounding a theory, which is an opinion or supposition based on reasoning from known facts. Your examination of such a theory will require five tasks:

1. Address the theoretical problem
2. Examine the literature
3. Classify the issues
4. Analyze and interpret the available data
5. Reach a conclusion on its social, psychological, and/or educational ramifications

Theoretical articles conform in general to this paradigm:

Introduction:
> Establish the theory and the problem it addresses.
>
> Discuss its background to establish its significance.
>
> Provide a review of literature on the theory, both the pro and the con.
>
> Offer a thesis sentence that addresses the problem to defend the theory, to anticipate a new theory, or to demonstrate that one theory has superiority over another.

Body:
> Classify and explain in detail the issues.
>
> Compare and contrast two or more theories or the issues of one.
>
> Develop a past-to-present progression to trace the development of the theory.
>
> Provide quotations and paraphrases of experts who have addressed this problem in the literature.

Conclusion:
> Discuss and defend your ideas as they develop from the evidence in the body.
>
> Offer a new theory.
>
> Defend the merits of one theory over another.
>
> Suggest problems that might need additional study.

You will need to pick and choose from the options listed above. As the writer, you must develop your own arrangement, using the paradigm as a guide to elements that may or may not fit your design.

For example, one student examined the theory behind the practice of genocide by the Nazis and applied it to practices in modern America. The task first required careful reading, the citation of the literature, and analysis and evaluation of both the theory and its improper applications in contemporary society. The paper is reproduced next.

Model 1: A Theoretical Report in APA Style

Genocide 1

Running head: GENOCIDE

Genocide: The Expanding Parameters

Cathy M. Meriweather

Honors English 1010
Professor Lock
November 20, 1998

Genocide: The Expanding Parameters

Cathy's opening establishes the theory about an apathetic public.

When a group of people has been singled out for extermination, the act has historically been preceded by an organized campaign to dehumanize the subject by means of propaganda to separate them from the rest of the human race. The victimizer appeals to mankind's tendency for bigotry, stirring the masses with outrage and self-pity, securing their subject as the object of scorn, and undermining the collective conscience. They are beguiling killers. Only by lowering public esteem for the select group can the killers rationalize their heinous plot; they offer it to an apathetic public as a reasonable solution to a perceived threat or an unwanted burden. In this way the seeds of hate are sown, destined to mature into the bitter

She cites literature to defend her stance.

fruit of genocide. For example, MacKinnon (1993) has demonstrated that the Serbs' campaign to gain ethnic cleansing has used rape against women as a war tactic. The Serbs have filmed many of the rapes and used the evidence as pornographic propaganda to depict the Croats (the victims) as somehow subhuman and therefore worthy of extermination.

Johansen (1996) has asked the pertinent question: "Can we do nothing?" He condemns the world community for its inadequate protection of the ethnic groups in Rwanda and Yugoslavia. Landau (1994) pinpointed the apathy of the United Nations

organization, which has done nothing to prosecute
known criminals in Yugoslavia. Landau adds, "History
suggests that no action will be taken" (p. 8). Too
often, bystanders merely observe, perhaps wring their
hands, but do nothing. Hilberg (1992) examined this
phenomenon in his recent book, <u>Perpetrators, Victims,
Bystanders: The Jewish Catastrophe, 1933-1945</u>.

Today, we are the bystanders to a new group of
victims in the United States. This group consists of all
Americans who suffer the misfortune of being
unwanted by their parents or, worse, of being merely
inconvenient (as in, "It's just not convenient to have
a baby right now"). Abortion and related actions, such
as fetal tissue research, are new forms of genocide. We
are again testing the theory that bystanders will
ignore genocide to leave a class of humans
unprotected.

To understand how a civilized society can be led
into such a crime, we must attempt to identify our
own susceptibility to mass deceit. When we accept the
devaluation or destruction of another human group by
not voicing objections, then we share in the guilt of the
killers. Milgram's study (1975) showed shocking
evidence that many people, submitting to a strong
dictator, would murder a fellow human being. More
recent studies have reinforced Milgram's argument.
Luttwak (1993) has even suggested that if the

Cathy turns the theoretical essay into an argument. She explores the general theory that the great mass of the populace wishes to be indifferent to the suffering of others.

Here Cathy advances her thesis in light of the theory that has been advanced.

Genocide 4

Bosnians were only dolphins they would receive far more protection than they currently do. Could the same be said about the human fetus?

How do the powerful gain an advantage over an oppressed class? The subhuman or nonhuman status of the unborn child is constantly reinforced with generic names such as <u>zygote</u>, <u>embryo</u>, and <u>fetus</u>. However, to borrow from Shakespeare, is not a rose by any other name still a rose? Unfortunately, with a propaganda machine in place, every bit as sophisticated as the Nazis, the conscience of the American public is saturated and, in part, corrupted. The propagandists portray a human being as a parasite attaching itself to a superior life, an organic blob of tissue, like a cancer, fit only to be removed and disposed of.

When does random killing or mass murder become genocide? "Prior to 1944 the term did not exist. It was coined by the Polish legal scholar Raphael Lemkin to describe what was happening to the Jews in Nazi occupied Europe" (Porter, 1982, p. 2). Since then, a more general definition has been: the deliberate annihilation of an entire group of people (Porter, 1982, pp. 8-9). To be identified as a "group," there must exist a unifying characteristic of all members in the group, such as religion, race, political affiliation, or ethnic identity. In the mid-1930s, Adolf Hitler

---

Cathy uses questions to confront the reader and set up her answers.

Cathy's paper is personal even though it is theoretical. She has brought her own background and experience to the assignment, using it as an opportunity to voice her perception that the pro-choice group is engaged in a liberal propaganda blitz.

began to advance his plan for the destruction of
European Jews. Launching a massive propaganda
campaign with the objectives of instilling fear and hate
against the Jews, he used such words as vermin, lice,
parasites, rodents, filthy animals, racial pollutants, and
degenerates. These labels began the process of
dehumanization. The fact that the Nazis considered the
Jews non-human was appropriately demonstrated by
the use in the gas chambers of Z gas, "a chemical
developed for the killing of rodents" (Porter, 1982, p.
14).

Helen Fein (1978) has explained that this process
"legitimizes the existence of a state of folk as a
vehicle for the destiny of the dominant group and, by
definition, excludes the victim-group [non-volk] as
being outside the realm of the 'sanctified univers e'
. . . without a claim to the human race" (cited in
Porter, 1982, pp. 13-15). The public acceptance of this
ideology was made easier by a reinforcing propaganda
of flattery that alleged Aryans to be racially superior.
The crescendo of Hitler's plan was the "final
solution" to the "Jewish problem"—the annihilation of
all the Jews in Europe. The fact that killing on such a
grand scale is unlikely to go unnoticed was apparently
not worrisome to the Nazi regime. Because of their
mastery of the art of information manipulation, they
knew that the more outrageous the reports of

The body of
her paper
gives back-
ground infor-
mation on the
Nazi regime.
She thereby
traces a past-
to-the-present
progression.

Cathy avoids
the technical
jargon of the
subject to
focus on the
social impli-
cations.

atrocities were, the less likely people were to believe them. Conversely, the more preposterous a lie is, the more believable it becomes.

As in Nazi Germany, the expediency of the death of a "zygote" is far more important than the suffering of the victim, so perhaps, like the Nazi regime, the propagandists are aware that the atrocity of their crime is far too horrible to be quickly absorbed or admitted into the public awareness. In short, if our attitudes about life are not reformed, the size of this victim group can be expected to expand dramatically. Extermination of the unwanted unborn will ultimately be only a natural predecessor to the extermination of the unwanted elderly or the unwanted terminally ill. Towards this end, new devices for death have already been test marketed by such pioneers as Dr. Jack Kovorkian, and with certainty others will follow. Our generation, in a nation void of empathy, where the sanctity of life is forgotten, will one day find itself in the same victim group that we failed to protect. Then it will be our dismemberment for organ harvesting, our corpses rendered for cosmetics, and our pain that an apathetic America ignores.

Staub (1996) made the connection between genocidal violence and the violence in today's teenagers. He has shown that frustration and unfulfilled needs will cause violence. In particular, poverty and desperation will cause scapegoating. And we know what happens to the scapegoat, whether he or she is a Jew, a Croat, or an unborn child.

In theory, the disinterest of the bystanders makes possible a modern genocide of gigantic proportions. In theory, apathy reigns. It does not have to be this way!

Cathy's conclusion drives home the telling point—genocide is not confined to history. The apathy continues.

References

Hilberg, R. (1992) <u>Perpetrators, victims, bystanders:
The Jewish castrophe, 1933-1945.</u> New York: Aaron
Asker.

Johansen, R. C. (1996). Will we do nothing?
Preventing genocide. <u>The Christian Century, 113,</u>
316-319.

Luttwak, E. N. (1993, October). If Bosnians were
dolphins. <u>Commentary, 96,</u> 27-33.

Landau, R. (1994). Never again? <u>History Today, 44,</u> 6-
8.

MacKinnon, C. A. (1993, July-August). Turning rape
into pornography. <u>Ms, 4,</u> 24-31.

Milgram, S. (1975). <u>Obedience to authority.</u> New York:
Harper & Row.

Porter, J. N. (1982). <u>Genocide and human rights.</u>
Lanham, MD: University Press of America.

Staub, E. (1996). Cultural-societal roots of violence:
The examples of genocidal violence and of
contemporary youth violence in the United States.
<u>The American Psychologist, 51,</u> 117-133.

Proposals and Reports on Empirical Research

Empirical research means the gathering of knowledge as based on observation or experiment, not on theory. Therefore, a written report about your original research will be an *empirical study*. It will introduce your hypothesis, explain in detail your methods for proving or disproving the hypothesis, report the findings, discuss the findings, and interpret the implications of your research. In the report of empirical research you will draw upon existing literature in your introduction to establish the scholarly nature of your work and use it sometimes in the conclusion to endorse and lend credence to your discussion at the end of the paper. The heart of the study will be your original research, which might take the form of a test, questionnaire, or observation of the experimental group. The object is to gather data that will show the validity of the hypothesis.

For example, one student began with this hypothesis: Control of criminal activity is hampered by the police workload on non-criminal matters. She developed a research proposal that addressed these questions:

What is the problem?
Is the problem worthy of study?
Will the study have significance?
What literature is available on the subject?
Can you frame a hypothesis?
Must you define terms, make assumptions, set limitations?
How will you design the study in order to collect data?
Will the results have reliability and validity?

In many cases, the research proposal will constitute the finished product (see the sample essay 35–43). In other cases, the task will require students to conduct the original research within the city's police department. In this case, she selected a set of subjects at random from among the active officers on the police force. She planned and executed a period of observation and personal contact with them and tabulated the statistics. With the empirical data in hand, she was prepared to develop her report in accord with the following general paradigm:

Abstract
Introduction
    The problem
    The hypothesis
    The background (including pertinent literature)
    The purpose and rationale with a brief summary of what
        the research entailed
Method (the experimental design)
    Subjects
    Apparatus
    Procedure
Results
Discussion
References

The **abstract**, which is usually written last, is a brief summary of the project. In about 100 words you must explain the problem and your hypothesis, describe your basic method or design, summarize the results, and announce briefly the conclusions or implications of the study. A reader should be able to comprehend the essence of your study merely by reading the abstract. (See page 35 for a sample abstract.)

In the **introduction** you will explain the problem and the manner in which the experimental design will test or defend the hypothesis. Explain the purpose of your work and your reasons for conducting the test or observation. The introduction must also cite pertinent literature and establish the relationship between previous and present research. Close the introduction with a brief summary of what you did in your investigation of the hypothesis.

To help in composing the introduction, you might consider these matters:

1. What problem am I examining?
2. Have I framed the hypothesis to address the problem?

3. How does my work relate to previous research?
4. What are the implications of the study?

If your introduction answers these questions, your reader will comprehend the nature of the research.

The **method** section requires you to explain the design of your work, usually in three sections to name the subjects, to itemize the apparatus, and to describe the procedure. The method section must be thorough so that other researchers might replicate your work. That is, you must explain *what* you did and *how* you did it. If appropriate, identify the subjects. Who participated? Were the subjects randomly selected? How did you select them? What are their general demographics, such as age and sex? You must also name precisely your apparatus, such as equipment, furniture, stopwatch, photographs, tapes, and so forth, even to the point of giving brand names. The procedure section describes your selection, formation, and experimental manipulations of the subjects. That is, tell your readers what you did.

The **results** section provides a summary of your findings. Include data that run counter to your hypothesis. If appropriate, provide charts, figures, and statistical tables. However, do not elaborate or discuss the facts; save your analysis for the next section.

The **discussion** section interprets and evaluates the implications of your work.

What does your study contribute?
Does it address and answer the problem?
Did it prove the hypothesis?
What conclusions can you reach?
What are the wider implications of the results?

By answering these questions, your discussion will explain the findings in light of the original hypothesis, which is verified by the study, is subject to modification, or is unsubstantiated. Note: mention negative findings without dwelling on every flaw and without extreme efforts to explain them away. If appropriate, relate your work to previous studies on the problem. The discussion should also mention any theoretical or practical consequences of the study.

Reference citations must be provided to document your comments on the literature. Every mention of a source in your text demands an entry on the reference page, and every entry on the reference page must be mentioned in the text (see *Writing Research Papers*, sections 10d and 10g).

Other material—graphs, charts, samples of letters and questionnaires—should be placed in an appendix at the end of the paper.

Model 2: A Research Proposal in APA Format

Communication Skills 1

Running Head: EFFECTS OF COMMUNICATION SKILLS

The Effects of Communication Skills
on Development of Constructive
Interpersonal Relationships

Julie A. Strasshofer
Austin Peay State University
May 4, 1998

Abstract

Marital and premarital counselors have used communication skills training on a regular basis to enhance the couple's relationship. This study explores the effects of using a similar type of communication training model on an adolescent's ability to develop constructive relationships with close friends and family members. It is hypothesized that giving in-class instruction to Tennessee high school students on how to proficiently express themselves and listen to others will enhance the quality of their interpersonal relationships as measured by a revised version of the Interpersonal Relations Questionnaire (IRQ). The expected results of this study and its limitations are discussed.

The abstract gives a brief overview of the report.

The hypothesis is that in-class instruction on how adolescents can proficiently express themselves and listen to others will enhance the quality of their interpersonal relationships.

Communication Skills 2

The Effects of Communication Skills

on Development of Constructive

Interpersonal Relationships

The ability of a person to interrelate with others in personal, as opposed to public, relationships has been a very important aspect of societal structures. There is a concern that the breakdown of the American family has lead to a breakdown of the American society leading to crime, violence, and a decay in moral values. Since the family structure depends highly upon the relationship of husband and wife, a breech in that relationship can destroy the family unit. Gottman, Markman, and Notarius (1977) have found that poor communication between a husband and wife can lead to marital distress and possibly separation of the marriage partners. Markman and Hahlweg (1993) suggested the teaching of communication skills to married couples before problems arise in order to decrease marital distress.

This concept has carried over into the realm of premarital counseling. Numerous churches extending across the denominations have come to require premarital counseling weighted heavily with communication skills in order to prevent distressed marriages and to decrease divorce rates. This practice has also been studied and recommended by Markman, Renick, Floyd, Stanley, and Clements (1993);

Julie uses *and* between names of the sources in the text, but she will use & in the list of references.

In the *introduction* Julie examines the issue, discusses literature on the topic, and advances the hypothesis.

Communication Skills 3

however, none of these studies explore the possibility of teaching these skills to adolescents before they become involved in serious relationships or what effect this may have on other types of close relationships.

Other types of close relationships include those of parent-child, sibling-sibling, and same-sex friendships. Riesch, Tosi, Thurston, Forsyth, Kuenning, and Kestly (1993) found that when proper communication skills taught to adolescents and their parents were used within the family structure, they "decreased antisocial" attitudes and encouraged "openness to resolving" conflicts (p. 15); thus, they created more satisfying family relationships. These skills should also produce similar effects in other unions including close friendships. Samter (1992) tied certain types of communication habits together with lonely people, which once again supports the importance of communication on the quality of a relationship.

The ability of a person to interrelate with others in social and intimate settings begins as a child learns to interact with others either by observation, or by instruction, and then continues to develop throughout life. Even though this acquisition of knowledge steadily increases in childhood, many young adults are not sufficiently prepared to deal with the types of social interaction which face them as they proceed through adolescence and young adulthood. Since effective

Communication Skills 4

communication has an important role in relationships, and since relationships have such an impact on society, then the effects of training communication skills to adolescents should be further examined.

Here she explains the proposal and the hypothesis that it will examine.

This study has been designed to test the hypothesis that training Tennessee high school students in the applied use of communication skills, including definition of their opinions and emotions, accurate expression of these opinions and emotions, and the courteous reception of other's opinions and emotions, will enable these students to develop healthy and constructive interpersonal relationships as measured by a revised version of the Interpersonal Relations Questionnaire (IRQ).

Method

Julie builds the *method* section by explaining the subjects for the proposed observation, the testing instruments to be used, and the procedure to implement the study.

Subjects

The subjects will consist of high school students in grades 10, 11, and 12. They will be selected from high schools in and around Nashville, Tennessee, through contact with principals by letter requesting their school's participation in this study. Only those schools which have a mandatory Health or Wellness class will be accepted because interpersonal relationship is a relevant issue to the student's mental and emotional well being, and the unit will not distract from the course objectives.

The qualified respondents will then be separated

into 3 groups based on the socioeconomic status
(SES) of the school districts. Category 1 includes
poverty level through lower-middle class; Category 2
includes average-middle class; and Category 3
includes upper-middle class and above. One school
from each category will be randomly selected for the
study. Two classes from each school will be used for
the study, thus allowing for a control group and a
treatment group at each school. Any students
younger than 16 or older than 18 years of age will
be treated the same as the others in their groups, but
their scores will be disqualified from this study.
Reasons for this exception will be explored in the
discussion section.

<u>Instrumentation</u>

Characteristics of the students' interpersonal
relationship will be measured by using a test based on
the standard IRQ. This test measures personal
adjustment in adolescents aged 12 to 15 and will be
adjusted for 16- to 18-year-olds.

An open-ended questionnaire will also be developed
to inquire about the student's perceived quality of
past and present relationships. It will question such
things as average length of past and present
relationships, satisfaction of communication in family
and friendly relationships, along with the ability to
solve conflicts verbally. It will also inquire

Communication Skills 6

as to whether a student has noticed a change in his or her ability to communicate since taking the course.

Procedure

Communication skills will be taught to 1 class from each of 6 schools for 6 weeks, preferably when the students return from Christmas break. This will allow the students time to develop relationships during the school year prior to skill training, and also allow time after the training, but before the school year ends for students to notice tendency changes in their relationships.

The skills taught will be based on those used in a similar study by Riesch et al. (1993), but stressing areas concerning the definition and expression of feelings and opinions, along with listening techniques. These skills will not be family based as in the study by Riesch et al., but it will be focused toward those strategies used in a variety of interpersonal relationships.

The IRQ will be administered to all 6 classes prior to any training. The training sessions will be administered by a trained instructor and will be done carefully along specified guidelines in order to cover the same material in each classroom. At the end of the 6-week period, the 6 classes will once again take the IRQ. The open-ended questionnaire will be administered to all classes at the completion of the school year.

Students may also receive regular classroom tests at the discretion of the teacher for his or her use but will not be used in this study.

Results

The IRQ pretest and post test scores from the treatment group will be compared first with the control group from the same school; then, the treatment and control group means will be compared to their respective groups in the other categories; finally, the sum mean of all the treatment group scores will be compared to the sum mean of all control group scores.

The open-ended questionnaires will be examined for pattern changes and perceived changes in relationship quality. The results between treatment and non-treatment groups will be compared in order to examine whether any changes or trends could be related to normal maturation. The results will also be compared to the IRQ results in the attempt to expose any sensitivity created by pretesting.

Discussion

A positive correlation between communication and constructive interpersonal relationships is expected; however, the strength of the true correlation may differ from the test results due to limitations in the study. Some schools may not be selected randomly and the students may be already grouped according

She has no actual results because this work is a proposal.

She does describe how the scores and questionnaires will be tabulated for statistical data.

In the *discussion* she anticipates the correlations that might be found as well as the dangers of inaccurate results.

to school scheduling; therefore, any preassigned groups may be unique to the population and results may not remain consistent for all high school students in Tennessee. While SES is taken into account, other factors such as ethnic background, gender, and intelligence are not. All of these areas could be confounding, and could lead to inaccurate results. Also, as previously stated, a natural maturation is occurring quickly during this time in a person's life and influences changes in behavior or perception. Although the development of satisfying relationships in untrained adolescents is contrary to the research conducted by Riesch et al. (1993), eliminating the extremes adds a precautionary control. Other extremes, such as students who have been exposed to prior training in communication or students uninterested in learning, have not been controlled in this study but should be considered in future studies.

If the results of this study actually do show a positive correlation between communication skills and interpersonal relationships in the students tested, then consideration should be given toward refining this technique and using it in Wellness classes in an attempt to prepare adolescents in their development into young adults.

Communication Skills 7

References

Gottman, J., Markman, H., & Notarius, C. (1977). The topography of marital conflict: A sequential analysis of verbal and nonverbal behavior. <u>Journal of Marriage and the Family, 39,</u> 461-477.

Markman, H., & Hahlweg, K. (1993). The prediction and prevention of marital distress: An international perspective. <u>Clinical Psychology Review, 13,</u> 29-43.

Markman, H., Renick, M. J., Floyd, F. J., Stanley, S. M., & Clements, M. (1993). Preventing marital distress through communication and conflict management training: A 4- and 5-year follow-up. <u>Journal of Consulting and Clinical Psychology, 61,</u> 70-77.

Riesch, S. K., Tosi, C. B., Thurston, C. A., Forsyth, D. M., Kuenning, T. S., & Kestly, J. (1993). Effects of communication training on parents and young adolescents. <u>Nursing Research, 42,</u> 10-16.

Samter, W. (1992). Communicative characteristics of the lonely person's friendship circle. <u>Communication Research, 19,</u> 212-239.

Her references conform to APA style (see WRP-9, Section 10g).

The Review of Literature

In some instances the review article is a separate, independent work. In other cases, a brief review of the literature will be a part of the introduction to your research paper (see pages 1–2 of Julie's paper immediately above). In either case, you and your readers need to know what research has been done on the topic. It will explain the theoretical framework that ties together the various pieces of research literature. Thereby, it opens the door to your own research, which must grow from the previous research and from your present investigations. In this way, the new is linked to the old.

You will need a trilogy of reporting, interpreting, and evaluating. First, the review paper is a report, saying, in effect, here's a basic overview of the research on this problem. It gives a list of articles and books on the topic and it itemizes the findings and observations made by experts on the subject. Second, it provides a summary that interprets the various articles and books, that compares and contrasts their contributions in the light of current research, and that places each in the continuum of research on the specific problem. Third, the review of literature, by placing a work within the review, evaluates the research and shows its contribution to current theory.

The paradigm for a review of literature has these key divisions, though the divisions may not appear in the order shown:

Introduction
1. Identify the problem or hypothesis of the study.
2. Briefly summarize the problem so that your reader will understand the status of the ongoing research.

Body
1. Write a brief summary of each work to show how it contributes to research on the problem.
2. As you introduce each new work, compare and contrast it with previously mentioned literature.
3. Be certain that you interpret and evaluate each work's special contribution to research on the problem.

4. Identify relationships, discover gaps, and show any inconsistencies that you find.

Conclusion
1. Discuss the implications of the work in progress on the problem.
2. Explain how your work will be an extension of the existing work.

In effect, the review article provides an overview of research. It may serve as an isolated library assignment or as a prelude to your own research on the subject. (See also pages 78–80 for an example of the review of literature as a free-standing article.)

3 Writing a Research Paper in the Sciences

The sciences divide into two large groups, the natural sciences and the applied sciences. Natural scientists examine the earth and living things; applied scientists focus on technical and vocational applications. The disciplines therefore divide into these general groups, although they often overlap. Agriculture, for example, fits easily into both categories.

Natural Sciences	Applied Sciences	
agriculture	biomedicine	mathematics
biology	chemistry	medicine
botany	computer science	physics
geology	engineering	technology
zoology	health	

These groupings have importance to individual researchers who must adjust their goals and assumptions as well as their tools and methods of research. Even the standards of proof differ.

Natural scientists, for example, wish to discover, define, and explain the natural world. They work under the assumption that we can always gather new data about the soil in a pasture, the water in a local lake, or the cellular structure of the human heart. Physical scientists therefore perform objective analysis of the natural world by observing, testing, and cataloging data on flora and fauna, geological formations, animals, and many other things that compose this earth.

Applied scientists wish to apply the scientific knowledge that we possess to new arenas, so they introduce new strains of hybrid corn, they introduce in vitro fertilization, and they give us more sophisticated computers every year. Applied scientists discover drugs to control depression, they engineer more efficient engines, and they take caffeine out of coffee.

The Council of Biology Editors sets the standards in this academic area with its 1994 style manual, *Scientific Style and Format: The CBE Manual for Authors, Editors, and Publishers.* This manual advocates two citation and reference styles: (1) the name and year system for general biological studies and (2) the number system for bio-medical studies and research in the applied sciences. One or the other of these systems will serve your needs for most undergraduate papers (keeping in mind that your instructor may request that you conform to the style sheet of a journal to which you might submit your work). Therefore, use the CBE author-date format if you write a paper in any of the following disciplines: agriculture, biology, botany, geology, zoology (see pages 60–63). However, use the number system for papers in other scientific disciplines: bio-medicine, chemistry, computer science, engineering, health, mathematics, medicine, physics. (See below, 64–68).

Understanding the Writing Style for Papers in the Sciences

Scientific writing translates hard data, such as mathematical formulas and chemical symbols, into essay form. It explains how satellites in space beam their signals to earth. It documents the correlation between seismic signals and potential earthquakes. When you perform as the scientific writer, even as an apprentice in the field, you must understand the problem you wish to address, know the language of the discipline, and share the knowledge with colleagues and the public in a fluent, error-free prose. You will need to report the scientific data and interpret it objectively. Your discussion is simply not valid unless you base it on the findings, not on your subjective feelings.

Incorrect: I was disappointed to discover that my theory was invalid, even though I did everything right.

Correct: The data did not confirm the hypothesis.

Scientific writing does not mean just getting the facts straight. Even after you run an experiment perfectly and write out the facts, most instructors will want more from you, even in laboratory reports. They want your interpretation of the facts. They want you to demonstrate that you know what the results mean to the scientific community.

Remember, too, that the paradigm of scientific writing affects your style. In the introduction your voice will invite the reader to share a problem, understand the background, review previous work, and examine your findings. In the conclusion you will explore the meanings and consequences of the results, usually in active voice (i.e., "shell selection by hermit crabs is a specific process" or "further evidence of earlier ages needs to be found to confirm which form of pollination is most primitive"). However, in the methods and results sections in the middle of the report your voice must be factual and *you* as a speaker must retreat into the background by the use of the passive voice, which focuses attention on the research problem and the method, not on you, the researcher (i.e., "hermit crabs were collected," "morning collections were made"). A final "Comments" section will allow you to make subjective comments on what you have learned by conducting the experiment (see page 55 for an example).

One final note: in writing for a general audience, define technical terminology; however, in a laboratory report or the report of empirical research the technical jargon is appropriate without explanation.

Types of Papers in the Sciences

In general, and with variations, scientific papers appear as (1) a laboratory or field report, (2) a scientific analysis, or (3) a report of empirical research. These are explained below.

The Laboratory or Field Report

The laboratory or field report requires you to conduct an experiment in the laboratory or out in the field (i.e., a body of water, a rock formation, a corn field). Your task is two-fold: (1) to replicate (reproduce) an exercise that has been performed numerous times by other students (2) to write a report that explains with precision your results and—most importantly—your procedures for reaching the result. Many variables can influence your work, and the instructor is looking for your thoroughness in reporting the facts and what they mean, especially those elements that appear wrong to you or that differ from the expected results. In general, the form of the report will be dictated by the instructor who, in most cases, will ask you to use a workbook or work from hand-out sheets. Forms and formats will vary, but you will be asked to supply such items as these:

1. Title, experiment number, and date.
2. Introduction (describe the experiment; include literature consulted and the reasons for conducting the research).
3. Objective (describe briefly what you hope to accomplish).
4. Procedure (give details about the apparatus and the design of the experiment; you may be required to draw a picture of some items).
5. Results (give your findings, which will usually be statistics in tabular form).
6. Discussion of results (provide your interpretation of the data; use this section to understand the data and the reasons for conducting the experiment).
7. Comments (optional) on what you learned by the experience.

In some cases, your laboratory reports must be submitted in a notebook, which will require a title page and perhaps other matter as required by the instructor or by the experiment itself (i.e., a table of contents or an appendix).

Model 3: The Brief Laboratory Report

Christopher Armistead

Chemical Analysis

The Determination of the Acid Content
of Vinegars and Wine

Experiment 4

Introduction

The stomach produces gastric juice, an acidic
substance, when digesting food. In some cases, a
person's body produces too much gastric juice and
the acidity in the stomach is too high. If this person
were to eat foods with a high acidity, the stomach
problem would increase and sometimes cause ulcers or
other medical problems.

One way to prevent further damage to the body is
to limit or monitor the intake of acid. In order to do
this, a person would need a method of procedure to
determine the acidity of foods. This experiment is
useful because it estimates the acidity of a vinegar
and wine sample, thus enabling someone to regulate
their daily intake of acid.

Objective

The objective of this laboratory experiment is to
determine the acidity of a vinegar and wine sample.

Procedure

To begin, 25.0 ml of a vinegar sample was
delivered to a 250-ml volumetric flask, with a 25-ml
pipet, and diluted to the mark with distilled water. It

A descriptive
introduction
identifies the
problem—acidity in the stomach.

Christopher's
objective is
stated clearly
and simply—to
determine the
acidity of a
vinegar and
wine sample.
The writer's
procedure section is highly
detailed.

was mixed thoroughly and 50.00-ml aliquot were
emptied into three 250-ml conical flasks, with a 25 ml
pipet, 50 ml of distilled water, and two drops of
phenolphthalein were added to each of the flasks. The
samples were then titrated with a .345 M NaOH
solution until the first permanent pink color.

Next, 10 ml of aliquot was added to three conical
flasks, with a 10-ml pipet, 50-ml of distilled water, and
six drops of phenolphthalein were added to each of the
conical flasks. Then, the samples were titrated with a
0.120 M NaOH solution until the first permanent pink
color.

Christopher's
results sec-
tion supplies
statistics with
mean, range,
and *standard
deviation.*

Results

Vinegar	1	2	3
Init. Reading	0.00 ML	0.00 ML	0.00 ML
End Reading	34.20 ML	34.10 ML	34.00 ML
NaOH Added	34.20 ML	34.10 ML	34.00 ML
W / V %	4.93%	4.91%	4.90%

Mean: 4.91%
Range: 0.02%
Standard Deviation   0.0158
90% Confidence Interval   4.91% +/-0.0266

Wine	1	2	3
Init. Reading	0.00 ML	8.50 ML	15.20 ML
End Reading	8.50 ML	15/20 ML	22.20 ML
NaOH Added	8.50 ML	6.70 ML	7.00 ML
W / V %	0.765%	0.603%	0.630%

Mean: 9.666%

Range: 0.162%

Standard Deviation   0.071

90% Confidence Interval 0.666 +/- 0.119

Sample Calculations:

90% Confidence Interval: $X +/- \dfrac{ts}{\text{Sqrt. N}}$

Vinegar: $90\% \ CL = 4.91\% +/- \dfrac{(2.92)(0.0158)}{\text{Sqrt. 3}}$

$90\% \ CL = 14.13\% +/- 0.0266$

W/V%:V NaOH $\dfrac{\text{mol NaOH}}{\text{L NaOH}}$ $\dfrac{\text{1 mol AcOH}}{\text{1 mol NaOH}}$ $\dfrac{\text{fw AcOH}}{\text{1 mol AcOH}}$ = 9 AcOH

$\dfrac{\text{g AcOH}}{\text{total ml}}$ x 100 % = M1

M1 x 2 = M2

M2 x 10 = W/V % of vinegar

V NaOH $\dfrac{\text{mol NaOH}}{\text{L NaOH}}$ $\dfrac{\text{1 mol Ta(OH)}_2}{\text{2 Mol NaOH}}$ $\dfrac{\text{fw Ta(OH) 2g-gTa(OH)}_2}{\text{1 mol Ta(OH)}_2}$

$\dfrac{\text{g Ta(OH)}_2}{\text{total ml}}$ x 100 % = M1

M1 x 6 = W/V % of wine

Discussion

Customarily, the acid content of vinegar is reported in terms of acetic acid, even though other acids are present. Similarly, wine is expressed as a percent of tartaric acid, although other acids are present in the

The writer provides an ample supply of calculations.

Christopher's *discussion* examines the differences in his results from the norm. He itemizes three possible causes, including the change of personal errors in conducting his research.

sample. Usually, most vinegars contain about 5% acid (w/v) expressed as acetic acid; on the other hand, wine contains somewhat under 1% acid (w/v) expressed as tartaric acid.

The experimental results of the vinegar are similar, but the results of the wine do not correspond to the normal tartaric acid percentage. The wine sample's acidic percent is about half of the normal percentage.

A few factors could explain the differences in results. First, the experiment called for a .1 M NaOH standard solution but a 0.120 M NaOH solution was used instead, which may or may not matter.

Second, the concentration of the wine sample differs from that of the standard wine sample. In a standard wine sample, 50-ml of aliquot is added to 50-ml of distilled water forming a 1:2 ratio. This means there is one mole of aliquot for every two moles of water. In this experiment, 10-ml of aliquot is added to 50-ml of water, making a solution with a 1:6 ratio. There is one mole of aliquot for every six moles of water; hence, forming a more dilute solution. Because of this, it may take less NaOH base to titrate the wine sample than it takes to titrate a standard wine sample. This could explain why the tartaric acid percentage in the wine sample is lower than the acid percentage of the standard sample.

Third, there may have been personal errors involved because the experiment was performed carelessly. The sample concentrations may have been inaccurately made, and, over or under titration may have occurred. One or all of these factors may have influenced the test, hindering the results.

UNKNOWN NUMBER: 19

W/V OF ACETIC ACID IN VINEGAR: 5.24%

w/V OF ACETIC ACID IN WINE: 0.666

Comments

    This experiment was interesting because I saw how the acidity of home-made and store bought wine differ. I've always heard home-made wine is more stout or potent than store-bought wine, and this experiment proves it to be about twice as acidic.

The writer's comments reflect on the learning process.

Scientific Analysis

Scientific analysis requires you to explain a topic in detail by classifying parts, defining, showing process, comparing, and other techniques. It means that you might need to write a description that explains one of Edison's inventions, write an essay that explains the process of natural selection for one species of insect, or write a detailed definition of chlorine to justify its use in the purification of drinking water.

In effect, scientific analysis explores the *why* and the *how* of a subject, as well as the *what*. It examines causal relationships and depends heavily upon several methods of developments, such as classification, cause and effect, comparison, process analysis, and definition. See *Writing Research Papers,* pages 137–42 for a full discussion of these processes.

Scientific analysis needs an **introduction** that identifies the problem, explores the background and history of the subject, cites the literature on the subject, and explains the purpose(s) for additional study and examination of the phenomenon. The **analysis** in the body of the paper will examine each issue or each part of the subject with definition, cause-effect explanations, comparison and contrast, and detailed inquiry into the natural processes. The **conclusion** explains the status of the current scientific studies, advances reasons for continued research, and suggests possible findings to quell and replace speculation on the subject. A scientific analysis will have a form and style similar to the paper shown above in this booklet on pages 22–30.

The Report of Empirical Research

The report of empirical research requires originality on your part. You must design the project, implement it, and then write out your findings, whether you are testing a hypothesis in the botany laboratory, digging at a geology site, or creating a hybrid strain of sweet corn. Often called *original* research, it enables you to discover the exact nature of a subject, why and how it functions, and how it relates to its environment. Your experiment provides the primary evidence for your report. (Chapter 2, pages 17–45 in this booklet, explains this process in the social sciences and provides a sample proposal on pages 35–43).

Your written report must conform in general to a set order:

Abstract
Introduction
Methods
Results
Discussion
References

The **abstract** is a brief summary of the report in 50–100 words. It explains your motivation to explore a problem, how you conducted the research, and what you found. Examples are provided on page 35 of this booklet and on pages 116–17 and 293 of *Writing Research Papers*.

The **introduction** should explain the purpose of your work and advance the hypothesis you will prove or disprove. It usually features three divisions:

The problem. Explain the problem that your work will address and offer the hypothesis that governed your research. Explain the point of your work and describe your research strategy.

The scientific background. Cite other source materials to show how your work relates to previously published articles. In particular, build the background of the project as necessary to show what has been done before and how your work will add new data and new insight on the subject. See also "Review Article," 77–80.

The purpose and rationale. If you have not done so, state the hypothesis, its relevance to the subject, and how your work fits a theoretical framework that might prove or disprove the implications of the study. If we put it another way, you must explain with scientific exactness how your model answers a basic question, such as, how does the burning of woodlands revitalize the flora and fauna? How do beavers interact with the environment? This work almost always begins with a question (How have deer reacted to suburban developments?) and your hypothesis that will control the direction of your research (The deer population continues to increase dramatically because the deer have found a safe refuge in the suburbs).

The **method** section explains how you conducted the study. This section is vital for several reasons: (1) it shows how appropriate you were in scientific techniques, (2) it helps to validate your results, and (3) it gives other researchers the tools for replicating your study. Divide this part of your report into subdivisions appropriately labeled:

Subjects. Tell who participated, how many there were, and how you selected them. Ethical standards should govern your use of animals as well as humans.

Apparatus. Describe thoroughly but briefly the materials used and how you used them.

Procedure. Explain how you performed the experimental manipulations.

Caution: the method section must be thorough and exact so that other researchers might replicate (duplicate) your work.

The **results** section must itemize your finding. Give factual details without elaboration. You will discuss the implications in the next section. Supply all relevant results, even those that conflict with your hypothesis. Use figures, tables, charts, drawings, and other statistical methods to report your findings. Some findings may be placed in an appendix, but relevant data must be shown within the "results."

In the **discussion** you must evaluate and interpret the implications of your findings. In particular, show how the findings reflect and/or dispute your hypothesis. Remember that negative findings have validity. You may also draw inferences from the findings and suggest additional research that might further shed light on the problem. Readers should learn what you contributed to the solving of a problem.

Your **references** should provide full data to any citations made to the literature on the topic. For the form and style of these entries, see below in this booklet, 63–63 and *Writing Research Papers,* pages 293–302.

The next model provides a portion of a report of empirical research. Space does not permit the publication of the full essay.

Model 4: The Report of Empirical Research in CBE Name and Year Style

Michael Stancil

October 1998

Isolation of the Lyme Disease Spirochete
from Small Mammals at Land Between
the Lakes Natural Area

Michael Stancil's language is the appropriate technical wording for empirical research.

Lyme disease is an arthropod-borne zoonosis caused by the spirochete <u>Borrelia burgdorferi</u> and is transmitted by various ixodid ticks (Burgdorfer et al., 1993; Burgdorfer, 1994; Johnson et al., 1994). Various mammals and birds have been implicated as reservoir hosts (Anderson et al., 1993, 1997a, 1996b). However, <u>Peromyuscus leucopus</u> (the white-footed mouse) appears to be one of the most important hosts in maintaining the bacterium in nature (Levine et al., 1995). In endemic areas of the United States, particularly the New England region, evidence suggests that there may be a natural transmission cycle between the tick <u>Ixodes dammini</u> and the white-footed

In his text Michael refers to his sources by last name and year.

mouse (Anderson et al., 1993; Bosler et al., 1993; Levine et al., 1995). Donahue and colleagues (1997) have shown that <u>P. leucopus</u> is an efficient reservoir for infecting larval and nymphal <u>I. dammini</u>. Moreover, Anderson et al. (1996a) isolated <u>B. burgdorferi</u> from 111 of 237 naturally infected white-footed mice. They also found that approximately 75 percent of the mice were infected during the summer months and the prevalence of infection in the winter was usually less than or equal to 33 percent.

A large portion of the paper has been omitted to save space. See pages 33–43 for examples of *method, results,* and *discussion* sections in a scientific analysis.

Ticks are not only reservoirs or biological carriers of viruses, bacteria, and protozoa but also mechanical carriers of viruses, bacteria, and protozoa. This mechanical type of transmission is often called "infection through interrupted feeding" (Anderson, 1998, p. 46). For example, the mouth parts of ticks may become contaminated with pathogens which may be inoculated into healthy animals when the ticks move from one host to another. Magnarelli et al. (1996) suggested that the presence of B. burgdorferi in the anterior and posterior portion of the tick's digestive tract means that transmission may occur by feeding or by spirochetes entering skin tissues of the host after being excreted from the tick.

I suggest that in non-endemic areas for Lyme disease where the arthropod vector is unknown, efforts should be undertaken to examine the prevalence of infection in mammals as well as ticks. Anderson (1998) found that B. burgdorferi persists in rodents for relatively long periods of time, possibly from the time of infection until death. Further study is needed in order to determine whether Lyme disease is established in this area.

In the references section Michael documents the sources according to the CBE style (see *WRP,* pages 308–11 for additional discussion and examples).

Literature Cited

Anderson, J. F. 1998. Mammalian and avian reservoirs for <u>Borrelia burgdorferi</u>. Ann. New York Acad. Sci. 539:180-191.

Anderson, J. F., L. A. Magnarelli, W. Burgdorfer, and A. G. Barbour. 1993. Spirochetes in <u>Ixodes dammini</u> and mammals from Connecticut. Am. J. Trop. Med. Hyg. 32:818-824.

Anderson, J. F., R. C. Johnson, L. A. Magnerelli, and F. W. Hyde. 1996a. Culturing <u>Borrelia burgdorferi</u> from spleen and kidney tissues of wild-caught white-footed mice, <u>Peromyscus leucopus</u>. Zentrabl. Bakteriol. Hyg. A. 263:34-39.

Anderson, J. F., R. C. Johnson, L. A. Magnerelli, and F. W. Hyde. 1996a. Involvement of birds in the epidemiology of the Lyme disease agent <u>Borrelia burgdorferi</u>. Infect. Immun. 51:394-396.

Bosler, E. M., J. L. Coleman, J. L. Benach, D. A. Massey, J. P. Hanrahan, W. Burgdorfer, and A. G. Barbour. 1993. Natural distribution of the <u>Ixodes dammini</u> spirochete. Science 220:321-322.

Burgdorfer, W. 1994. Discovery of the Lyme disease spirochete and its relation to tick vectors. Yale J. Biol. Med. 57:515-520.

Burgdorfer, W., A. G. Barbour, S. F. Hayes, O. Peter, and A. Aeschlimann. 1993. Lyme disease—a tick-borne spirochetosis? Science 216:1317-1319.

Donahue, J. G., J. Piesman, and A. Spielman. 1997.

Reservoir competence of white-footed mice for Lyme disease spirochetes. Am. J. Trop. Med. Hyg. 36:92-96.

Johnson, R. C., G. P. Schmid, F. W. Hyde, A. G. Steigerwalt, and D. J. Brenner. 1994. Borrelia burgdorferi sp. Nov.: etiologic agent of Lyme disease. Inter. J. Syst. Bacteriol. 34:496-497.

Levine, J. F., M., L. Wilson, and A. Spielman. 1995. Mice as reservoirs of the Lyme disease spirochete. Am. J. Trop. Med. Hyg. 34:355-360.

Magnarelli, L. A., J. F. Anderson, C. S. Apperson, D. Fish, R. C. Johnson, and W. A. Chappell. 1996. Spirochetes in ticks and antibodies to Borrellia burgdorferi in white-tailed deer from Connecticut, New York State, and North Carolina. J. Wildl. Dis. 22:178-188

Using the Number System in the Applied Sciences

In the applied sciences and the medical sciences, a number replaces the name and year.

> Various mammals and birds have been implicated as reservoir hosts (1). However, <u>Peromyscus leucopus</u> (the white-footed mouse) has been identified (2) as one of the most important hosts in maintaining the bacterium in nature.

You may include the name of the source in this form:

> Donahue et al. (3) have shown that <u>P. leucopus</u> is an efficient reservoir for infecting larval and nymphal <u>I. dammini</u>.

After completing a list of references, assign a number to each entry. Use one of two methods for numbering the list: (1) arrange references in alphabetic order and number them consecutively (in which case, of course, the numbers will not appear in consecutive order in the text; or (2) forego an alphabetic arrangement and number the references consecutively as they appear in the text, interrupting that order when entering references cited earlier.

Writing Research Papers, pages 313–23, discusses all the variations about the number system. Let's look at a portion of Michael Stancil's report converted to the number system.

Model 5: A Report of Original Research in the Number Style

Michael Stancil

October 1998

Isolation of the Lyme Disease Spirochete from
Small Mammals at Land Between
the Lakes Natural Area

Lyme disease is an arthropod-borne zoonosis caused by the spirochete <u>Borrelia burgdorferi</u> and is transmitted by various ixodid ticks (1, 2, 3). Various mammals and birds have been implicated as reservoir hosts (4, 5, 6). However, <u>Peromyuscus leucopus</u> (the white-footed mouse) has been identified (7) as one of the most important hosts in maintaining the bacterium in nature. In endemic areas of the United States, particularly the New England region, evidence has suggested (7, 8, 9) that there may be a natural transmission cycle between the tick <u>Ixodes dammini</u> and the white-footed mouse. It has been shown (10) that <u>P. leucopus</u> is an efficient reservoir for infecting larval and nymphal <u>I. dammini</u>. Moreover, <u>B. burgdorferi</u> has been isolated (8) from 111 of 237 naturally infected white-footed mice. It has also been found (8) that approximately 75 percent of the mice were infected during the summer months and the prevalence of infection in the winter was usually less than or equal to 33 percent.

Michael has shifted the in-text citations to numbers and has omitted, in most cases, the name of the authority. The sense of the writing in the applied sciences is to keep the focus on the data, not the person or persons who have developed it. The names will be found on the Literature Cited page.

A large portion of the paper has been omitted to save space. See pages 35–43 for examples of *method, results,* and *discussion* sections in a scientific analysis.

Ticks are not only reservoirs or biological carriers of viruses, bacteria, and protozoa but also mechanical carriers of viruses, bacteria, and protozoa. This mechanical type of transmission is often called "infection through interrupted feeding" (8, p. 46). For example, the mouth parts of ticks may become contaminated with pathogens which may be inoculated into healthy animals when the ticks move from one host to another. It has been suggested (10) that the presence of B. burgdorferi in the anterior and posterior portion of the tick's digestive tract means that transmission may occur by feeding or by spirochetes entering skin tissues of the host after being excreted from the tick.

I suggest that in non-endemic areas for Lyme disease where the arthropod vector is unknown, efforts should be undertaken to examine the prevalence of infection in mammals as well as ticks. It has been discovered (8) that B. burgdorferi persists in rodents for relatively long periods of time, possibly from the time of infection until death. Further study is needed in order to determine whether Lyme disease is established in this area.

Literature Cited

1. Burgdorfer, W., A. G. Barbour, S. F. Hayes, O. Peter, and A. Aeschlimann. Lyme disease—a tick-borne spirochetosis? Science 1993;216:1317-1319.

2. Burgdorfer, W. Discovery of the Lyme disease spirochete and its relation to tick vectors. Yale J. Biol. Med. 1994;57:515-520.

3. Johnson, R. C., G. P. Schmid, F. W. Hyde, A. G. Steigerwalt, and D. J. Brenner. Borrelia burgdorferi sp. Nov.: etiologic agent of Lyme disease. Inter. J. Syst. Bacteriol. 1994; 34:496-497.

4. Anderson, J. F., L. A. Magnarelli, W. Burgdorfer, and A. G. Barbour. Spirochetes in Ixodes dammini and mammals from Connecticut. Am. J. Trop. Med. Hyg. 1993;32:818-824.

5. Anderson, J. F., R. C. Johnson, L. A. Magnerelli, and F. W. Hyde. Culturing Borrelia burgdorferi from spleen and kidney tissues of wild-caught white-footed mice, Peromyscus leucopus. Zentrabl. Bakteriol. Hyg. A. 1996a;263:34-39.

6. Anderson, J. F., R. C. Johnson, L. A. Magnerelli, and F. W. Hyde. Involvement of birds in the epidemiology of the Lyme disease agent Borrelia burgdorferi. Infect. Immun. 1996a;51:394-396.

7. Levine, J. F., M., L. Wilson, and A. Spielman. Mice as reservoirs of the Lyme disease spirochete. Am.

Notice that Michael has numbered the sources as he used them in the paper, thus the list of sources is *not* in alphabetical order. See pages 313–32 of *WRP* for details and variations on the number system, especially the shifts in usage from one discipline to another within the applied sciences.

J. Trop. Med. Hyg. 1995;34:355-360.

8. Anderson, J. F. Mamalian and avian reservoirs for
    <u>Borrelia burgdorferi</u>. Ann. New York Acad. Sci.
    1998;539:180-191.

9. Bosler, E. M., J. L. Coleman, J. L. Benach, D. A.
    Massey, J. P. Hanrahan, W. Burgdorfer, and A. G.
    Barbour. Natural distribution of the <u>Ixodes
    dammini</u> spirochete. Science 1993;220:321-322.

10. Donahue, J. G., J. Piesman, and A. Spielman.
    Reservoir competence of white-footed mice for
    Lyme disease spirochetes. Am. J. Trop. Med. Hyg.
    1997;36:92-96.

4 Writing a Research Paper in the Humanities

Humanists examine, among other things, human experience in history, human values in literature (poetry, fiction, drama), and human-made beauty in works of art (painting, sculpture, music, film). They work in the fields of history, fine and applied arts, English, philosophy, and religion. Humanists accept a poem or a painting as a valid entity and search subjectively for what it means to human experience. In contrast, a scientist focuses on a small set of data, and with other scientists develops a valid model, design, or structure, such as a new stethoscope, a new view of Mars, or a better reading of water pollution in the Everglades.

Scientist: Water temperature affects the germination of hermit crabs.

Humanist: Water imagery in the fiction of D. H. Lawrence suggests rebirth.

As shown above, a scientist spends time explaining procedures and the methods used for testing a hypothesis (see pages 9–10),

69

but the humanist goes directly into interpretation that defends a thesis statement.

The typical paradigm for a paper in the humanities has three basic parts:

- Identify the subject and express a thesis
- Analyze the subject
- Interpret it in light of the thesis

Accordingly, the humanist will assume (1) that the historical record is valid and go forward with the analysis or will assume (2) that the work of art is whole and complete and go forward with the interpretation. At other times, the humanist will attempt to fill the gaps in the record, identify a newly discovered work of art, make a correction to a biased historical record, or examine an original manuscript that differs with a published version.

Writers in philosophy examine moral, ethical, and legal issues. Historians examine causes for events and their effects on society at the time and on future generations. Writers who examine literature and the fine arts look for meanings, themes, and messages as conveyed by a song, a painting, or a story.

These interpretations of history, philosophy, and works of art are not judged *right* or *wrong* or referred to as *positive results* or *negative findings*. They will be judged instead by the readers within the academic community by how reasonable and valid the interpretation is in its social applications. Thus, Willa Cather's fiction can be subjected to a feminist study, a historical interpretation, and a symbolic reading. The proof of the humanist's argument lies within the work itself, so the interpretation must cite Cather's fiction with care and draw support from other published interpretations.

When writing a paper in a field of the humanities, therefore, you must choose a narrowed topic that challenges your imagination and applies your contemporary point of view. Then you must address the issue seriously, asking "What is the problem?" "Who cares?"

Topic:	Newspaper comics
The problem:	Can the "funnies" speak on social, political, and psychological issues?

The audience:	People who have an intellectual curiosity about humor.
Topic:	Satire of the presidency in popular culture.
The problem:	Does criticism have redeeming values?
The audience:	People who have an intellectual curiosity about satire or about the presidency.

Using the topic of satire of the presidency, the historian might examine the role of presidential satire through the ages. Critics of modern culture might examine the satire of a comic strip, a cartoon, or a song. The philosopher might interpret the manner in which a newspaper column reflects the changing values of the public.

After you identify a problem, you need to frame a thesis sentence, which is a proposal to the reader, one that makes a critical approach to social, historical, ethical, and artistic theory. Rather than a scientific *hypothesis* that a scientist tries to prove with laboratory experiments or findings in the field, a humanist advances a *thesis*, which is a theory that the humanist will support with evidence from the primary source, be it historical documents, a drama by Shakespeare, or a sculpture by Rodin. Thesis sentence:

> Political satire of the presidency is valid, but insults of the sitting president's personal life are petty, political cheap shots hidden within comic strips.

The next thesis sentence sets the critical approach for the paper to explore the historical role of Aquinas.

> A great scholar of the Middle Ages, Thomas Aquinas, through his ability to systematically dissect and evaluate many pertinent questions, provided a theological foundation upon which the Catholic Church could build.

After locating a problem and framing a thesis sentence, you can widen your scope with an exploratory visit to the library. If you read a few books and/or articles on the subject, you can narrow the topic to a specific issue.

Satire. An attempt to improve human society by blending wit and humor with criticism. Satirists ridicule social institutions in the hope of making people aware of their ludicrous shortcomings, and hence to correct them. The most effective and lasting *satire* is that which rises above personal invective and deals instead with universal types.

> —Martin Stevens and Charles H. Kegel,
> *A Glossary for College English*

One writer used this source to frame this thought:

Political cheap shots usually fail because "lasting satire . . . rises above personal invective" to touch upon universal issues of national concern.

In addition to consulting sources, humanists talk with other people to learn more about a topic. Humanists are concerned about what people think and how they respond to events and to works of art. You also should talk with fellow students and interview knowledgeable adults. (Various techniques for finding source material are discussed on pages 5–15.)

Understanding the Writing Style of the Humanities

Several conventions will control your style and format in the areas of language, literature, philosophy, history, and art.

The present tense. First, verb tense distinguishes a paper in the humanities from one in the natural or social sciences. Humanists use the present tense when referring to previous works in the field ("Robert Frost says" or "the historian William Manchester states" or "the sculptures of Michelangelo express"). Scientists use the past tense or the present participle to refer to previous research in the field ("Einstein discovered" or "Finch and Wallace have observed").

The reason for this difference is found in the posture of the researchers. Scientists want to define a minute piece of scientific data that, when accomplished, has defined a particular model, formula, or data set. Thus, the scientist *has shown* or *has demonstrated* a fact. Humanists, on the other hand, make universal assumptions, so they use the historical present tense ("Charles Dickens *writes*" or "the music of Beethoven *expresses*"). The presentation of art and the interpretation of art continues into the present. Nobody has proved it; instead, it exists and remains subject to interpretation and evaluation.

Omitting the date. In addition, humanists are not too concerned about the date of scholarly interpretations. Arthur Symons's interpretation of Oscar Wilde's poetry has as much validity today as it did at the turn of the century; therefore, humanists say, "Arthur Symons *offers* this view" or "Arthur Symons *states*" without necessarily giving the date of the statement. Good ideas in the humanities are never considered out of date, unlike the sciences, where a theory may be superseded within a few years. MLA style and footnote style therefore require that you use the present tense in the text without an obligation to mention the year. In the bibliographic entry or the footnote, however, you must show the year.

Using the footnote system. The fine arts, history, and philosophy (but not literature) employ traditional footnotes, which should conform to standards set by *The Chicago Manual of Style*, 14th ed., 1993. With this system, use superscript numerals within the text, (like this[9]), and write a footnote at the bottom of the page, like this:

---

[28]Butterfield, <u>AFC</u>, 31 March 1976, 370.

[29]Ms. Gelles qtd. by Morris in <u>Seven Who Shaped Our Destiny: The Founding Fathers as Revolutionaries</u> (New York, 1973), 84. She also commented that the word "feminism" was not used until the late nineteenth century.

See *Writing Researh Papers,* section 11c, pages 324–32, for full details about writing footnotes and endnotes.

Writing a references page if one is required. At the end of your research paper, on a separate sheet, prepare a page that lists all sources mentioned in your paper. If you use the *Chicago Manual* footnote style, you may omit the separate references page because each of your footnotes will give the full bibliographic information. Note: check with your instructor about this requirement; some instructors require the bibliography in addition to the footnotes.

Writing Various Types of Papers in the Humanities

You will need to know the basic form and style for several types of papers in the humanities. The *summary* is a brief overview of selected material—a paragraph, a section, a chapter, and sometimes an entire article. The *review article* is an in-depth examination of an article or book, one that not only summarizes the work but also explains and interprets it. The *review of literature* summarizes and compares several different works that treat the same subject. The *research paper* is a lengthy examination of a subject.

The Summary
Also known as a *précis,* the summary captures in just a few words the ideas of an entire paragraph, chapter, article, or book. You will need the summary to annotate a bibliographic entry, to provide a plot summary, to create an abstract of our own paper, and to write a review article.

Put another way, writing a summary, like writing an abstract in the sciences, tests your ability to discover the relevant issues, which are those ideas in the article that enlighten you and will inform others about the subject. It asks you to examine and quickly summarize the essential nature of a work of art, whether it be novel, sculpture, or music. For example, an instructor in art history might ask you to write a précis of an article on the Pre-Raphaelite artist Millais; you would need to capture in just a few sentences the essential message of the article and perhaps add a sentence that addresses its contribution to art history. An extensive interpretation is usually reserved for the review article (see below).

Summarizing a 12-page article, one student wrote this summary:

Model 6: Summary

> One authority of this period argues that John Everett Millais, who founded the Pre-Raphaelite Brotherhood in 1848, was less a brother and less a rebel than his fellow painters, especially in comparison to Dante Gabriel Rossetti.[1] He cites Millais's return to traditional academic painting as evidence that Millais may have been caught up in the fervor of the movement but never committed himself wholly. Nevertheless, Millais provided the movement with some of its greatest works, including <u>Christ in the House of His Parents</u>.[2]

This summary gives a quick overview of an article about John Everett Millais. It captures the essential message, which identifies Millais's stature as a Pre-Raphaelite painter who never made a total commitment to the movement. The summary need not go beyond a paragraph of this type. To do so would be the creation of a critical review, which is discussed below (pp. 77–80).

Summary: The Annotated Bibliography

In another situation your summary may take the form of an annotated bibliography. This work will ask you to write a bibliographic entry (see pages 97–99) and follow it immediately by a summary of the work. Here's an example.

Model 7: Annotated Bibliography

> Pollak, Ellen. *The Poetics of Sexual Myth: Gender and Ideology in the Verse of Swift and Pope.* Chicago: U of Chicago P, 1985. The author investigates the sexual attitudes of Swift and Pope. She argues that even as women were progressing in the interests of their education during the 18th century, the exclusive and

> rigid categories of angel and whore remained intact in the writings of the period. Chapters 5 and 6 are of particular interest because they deal directly with Swift.

The writer provides a bibliography entry and follows it immediately with the annotation, which is her description and explanation of the work's focus on her subject—Swift's maligning of women. She does not drift into other matters so that the annotation maintains her focus on misogyny.

Plot Summary

In another case, you might need to summarize the plot of a story or novel or long poem. This task requires you to read and experience the work, to identify the major movements or events in the narration, and to write then a summary that captures within a few words the essential nature of the work. Note: it can briefly narrate what happened, but many times it will offer critical commentary and insight about the author's general theme.

Model 8: Plot Summary

> Jude the Obscure by Thomas Hardy narrates the miserable life of Jude Farley, a young man who ambitiously pursues a college education only to find obstacles at every step toward academia. Instead, he spends his life as a brick and rock mason. Along the way he is tricked and deceived by his wife Arabella and made despondent by his cousin and sometimes lover, Sue Bridehead. His eventual death only confirmed the pessimism that Hardy built into this social commentary on marriage, civil law, and educational opportunities in his beloved England.

This writer, who used the summary in the introduction to a research paper on the novel, assumes that the reader has read the novel and only needs a few reminders. As a general rule, this type of plot summary is best because it reports the facts quickly and then allows the writer to move into interpretation and evaluation.

Review Article

You may need to write a complete review of a work, an art display, or a musical performance. That is, instead of a brief summary, you must explain the nature of the work, interpret it, judge it, and relate it to the larger issues.

Several note-taking steps must be followed. First, read and experience the work in question and jot down your first impressions. Two, identify the work's purpose and thesis (usually found in the preface of a book but not readily available for a performance). Three, decide how the artist has developed and explored the central thesis. Fourth, compose your notes into a comprehensive whole that follows this paradigm:

Identify the work under review.
Offer a brief summary in one sentence.
Explain the work's purpose and thesis.
Analyze briefly how the artist has developed his or her ideas on the subject.
Close with a sentence or two about the artist and perhaps the relevance of the work to social, political, historical, or artistic traditions.

Economy is a virtue with this assignment. A page or two will usually suffice for the review of a performance or article, but a book review might require greater length. An example follows.

Model 9: A Review Article

Ginger Shepard

English 1020

31 October 1998

The Self and Community in

Toni Morrison's <u>Beloved</u>

Winner of the 1988 Pulitzer Prize for Fiction, Toni Morrison's <u>Beloved</u> deals with the lives of former slaves in the aftermath of the Civil War. Sethe, the central character, must cope with the terrible reality of her desperate attempt to save her children from the horrors of slavery. Her attempt to move forward into a complete, self-actualized future is the tale Toni Morrison so eloquently renders.

Not only does Morrison confront the racial issue, she also creates a world predominantly filled with strong women who band together in a world dominated by men. This, Morrison claims, is in part due to the legacy of slavery in its destruction of the black family because of the selling of children and the inevitable separation which occurred in the slave business. She bases her tragic story on the actual events in the life of Margaret Garner, a former slave who killed one of her children in order to prevent the slave owner from taking it away. In similar manner, Morrison's Sethe is unwilling to face the separation and attempts to kill her children, her "best things," in order to free them from the evils of slavery. She kills one, but not all of

While the review article is not yet a research paper, Ginger nevertheless provides a thesis—Sethe must be made whole again psychologically after murdering her own child—and cites evidence from the novel to elaborate upon the thesis.

her children. In Freudian terms, Sethe is torn between her "id," representing her motherly instinct to nurture and protect, and the "super ego," which tells her that killing her children for any reason is wrong.

Later, separated from her community, Sethe faces the ghost of her murdered child, and the ghost begins to devour Sethe. Sethe must eventually acknowledge her need for others in order to find psychological wholeness.

The fragmented and alienated characters in many postmodern novels do not seek community but remain isolated in their own false sense of self-sufficiency. In Toni Morrison's Beloved Sethe must face the horror of her past before she can be made whole and become a part of the community. The community provides an important means of healing and restoration for Sethe; thus Morrison's ending differs from many postmodern novels in which the characters remain fragmented and alienated, without hope of joining the community. True membership in the community comes only as a result of characters coming to terms with the fragments from the past which make up their own identities and of characters openly embracing the complex identities of others in a mutually beneficial communal bonding.

Unable and unwilling to address the reality of her actions, Sethe pushes the memories of her baby's murder deep inside herself until, after eighteen years, Paul D arrives and provides a vehicle both for

Ginger goes beyond mere plot summary in order to interpret and evaluate the nature of Morrison's literary contribution and its place within postmodern fiction.

remembering and for sharing the burden of the memories. Sethe's few nostalgic memories cause her to feel guilt, and her shared past with Paul D, though horrifying, draws her to him in her need to be "re-membered" and made whole again. Paul D attempts to stir Sethe from dwelling on her destructive past. In so doing, Paul D and Sethe must accept the past of slavery and move on to a new hope. By knowing themselves and their past, they can embrace the community.

The reader also must examine his or her own identity and must respond to his or her own community. This is not a story to pass on; the reader must recognize that an honest and responsible "re-membering" of the past cannot be faced alone successfully. The psychological need for her community must be met and satisfied before Sethe can become a whole person.

The Review of Literature on a Subject

Sometimes, instead of reviewing a major primary work, such as a painting, musical piece, or novel, an instructor will ask you to review secondary articles and books on the work. A body of criticism will inevitably build up around a major work, so this task requires you to summarize current publications about the subject, to establish the context of scholarly work on the subject, and to determine, perhaps, areas of study still available.

Therefore, this paper will present a set of summaries in essay form for two purposes:

1. It examines and shows how each source addresses a subject so that you provide yourself and your readers with an overview of the criticism.
2. It organizes the articles and books into classifications as you identify, perhaps, image studies, feminist views, symbolic interpretations, and even those who have positive or negative views of the subject.
3. It enables you to find an approach of your own, one not taken by others.

For an example, see *Writing Research Papers*, pages 99–104.

The Research Paper

In some instances instructors will ask you to write a complete analysis on a research problem that demands six to ten pages. Common guidelines apply for all papers of this type. To start, you should report, interpret, and evaluate a work of art as you address the research question. These are typical problems:

What do the ancient Aztec sculptures reveal about religion of that civilization?

What are the ethical issues of medically assisted suicides?

Why is Hamlet the major character in *Hamlet*?

Why did the United States become locked into the Vietnam War?

Why does Faulkner use black humor in many of his stories?

This type of assignment asks you to respond as an intelligent, informed observer. It does not ask for knee-jerk opinion, but it does mean bringing your personal experience to bear on a work or a problem after a period of critical reading, observation, and contemplation. It recognizes the subjective nature of humanistic issues where many viewpoints may prevail about a given topic.

A text or a painting or a historical account is not found complete and whole; it will be developed in part by you and other viewers or readers. Your interpretation of history and art and performances will depend upon your subjective knowledge as well as your objective analysis. That's the reason we get so many different interpretations of the same work. As a viewer or a reader, you will seek a vision that will satisfy your comfort level. Consequently, your critical reading will give meaning to the text just as your viewing and judgment of a painting will give it meaning. With this type of assignment, instructors are testing your reasoned, objective response *as well as* your subjective response as based on your background, identity, and intuitive response. Thus, your lifestyle and your philosophical outlook lie somewhere in the center of your interpretation.

Of course, you must work from an informed base. Learn the conventions of art and you can make an informed judgment about a painting by Millais. Discover the major movements of history, and you can respond effectively to a period of upheaval, such as the breakup of the Soviet Union. Read the Bible and learn biblical theory so that you can discuss intelligently the book of Luke. Several strategies will serve your needs in writing this type of paper. First, express an initial response to the question or issue. This response will prompt your critical approach to the problem and help you to frame a thesis sentence:

> The remains of ancient sculptures from the Aztecs of
> Mexico show a religion that was dark and sacrificial.

These critical approaches will enable the writer to begin an interpretation of the sculptures.

Second, you may need to examine, define, and elaborate upon key words and phrases, as shown by these examples:

> The term <u>sculpture in relief</u> means that the sculpture is
> attached to or a part of a flat surface. It might be <u>true
> relief</u> in which the figure(s) stands out from the surface or
> <u>intaglio</u> in which the figure(s) is carved into the
> background.

After you have defined the words, apply them to the poet or the
work of art, and continue with your interpretation.

Third, you may need to approach the problem by addressing
conventions and genres. You may then explain the convention or
the genre in detail and apply it to the problem.

> Surrealism used the power of the unconscious mind to
> depict a new reality. Salvador Dali dominated this genre in
> the first half of the century.

Introduction. You must express your response to the problem so
that you can argue from a selected position. There is usually an
answer or solution; however, to convince the reader, you may, like
the writer immediately, want to establish the conditions necessary
to meet your solution and then show that these conditions exist.

Body. Every topic sentence of the body needs to assert one aspect
of your answer, followed by details, such as quotations from the
work, events of historical significance, or descriptions of a piece of
art.

Conclusion. Affirm the validity of your interpretation by references to the artist, his or her preferences, choices, and statements.
Try to show that you are in line and in harmony with the artist's
point of view as expressed within the work and within other
works by the artist.

MODEL 10: A Brief Research Paper in History

Bill Strasshofer

History 2040

February 20, 1998

Thoreau's Search:

A Historical Perspective

Thoreau's "Civil Disobedience" and <u>Walden</u> emerged as flagships for the American Romantic Period. Refusing to be fettered by conformity and to be subjected to the rules of an earlier period, Thoreau questions everything around him, especially the American government. Just as Coleridge had become disillusioned with France, the champion of freedom turned oppressor, so too is Thoreau disillusioned by America, a country which had "undertaken to be the refuge of liberty" yet had one-sixth of its population bound as slaves.[1] Thoreau is further disturbed by the war with Mexico and the apparent apathy of the American people, who are "sound asleep nearly half" the time.[2] It is about these perplexities and his examinations of them that Thoreau writes, attempting to find and to reveal the wrongs, or the evil, underlying these disturbing situations.

The writer carefully uses the words of Thoreau himself to establish the issues to be addressed.

|

Both the superscript number and the corresponding footnote must appear on the same page.

---

[1] Henry David Thoreau, <u>Walden and Other Writings by Henry David Thoreau</u>. (New York: Bantam, 1989), 88.

[2] Thoreau, 349.

Thoreau's displeasure is well expressed when he writes that "he cannot without disgrace be associated" with a government "which is the slave's government also. "[3] To claim a stand for freedom while allowing even a small portion of the population to be enslaved is indeed a contradiction. Thoreau realizes that a government that will enslave one group of people might just as easily enslave another. He already feels this is the case since whatever the majority decides the minority must abide. He writes that a "government in which the majority rule in all cases cannot be based on justice," because it refuses to allow an individual to act according to what he believes to be right.[4] He questions why every man has a conscience if he must yield it to the legislators.[5] Thoreau believes that if men were not oppressed and forced to relinquish their own good judgment, they could all reach a higher state or realm. Hoping to enlighten his readers to the seriousness of this oppression, Thoreau likens the American "standing government" to a "standing army," and warns against the threat that this "army" poses to the individual.[6]

Thoreau sees little salvation in the right to vote as a vehicle to express one's will. He sees this right

---

[3]Ibid., 88.
[4]Ibid., 86.
[5]Ibid.
[6]Ibid., 85.

Bill has given deep and serious thought to his historical reading in Henry David Thoreau's works. He carefully organizes his response to Thoreau's ideas on the government, the masses, on the role of the individual, and on the influence of nature. While he shows a sympathetic understanding of Thoreau's ideas, he is, at the same time, aware of their limitations and contradictions.

as frivolous, "a sort of gaming . . . with a slight moral tinge to it."[7] In his eyes, this act accomplishes little toward securing what is right because voting does not ensure anything. It is merely a feeble attempt to reveal what one desires. He encourages the reader to cast his "whole vote," not just a ballot, but their "whole influence."[8] This "whole vote" is what he attempts to do by refusing to pay his poll-tax and by, consequently, being thrown in jail.[9] Having stood up to this powerful government, which compels so many to yield to it, he realizes the strength behind the government is the population's fear of what it might do. Having no fear, and not desiring to be free of his cell, Thoreau sees the government as "half-witted" and being as "timid as a lone woman."[10] Instead of feeling repressed, he feels himself free from the government's hold. He might have joined Lord Byron in exclaiming, "brightest in dungeons, Liberty thou art!"[11]

A significant portion of this research paper has been omitted to conserve space.

---

[7]Ibid., 89-90.
[8]Ibid., 94.
[9]Ibid., 96.
[10]Ibid., 97.
[11]Lord Byron, George Gordon, "Sonnet on Chillon," The Mentor Book of Major British Poets, ed. Oscar Williams (New York: Penguin, 1963), 127.

Thoreau believed nature to be special, something pure, not at the level of common man. It was something above a common man's comprehension. Nature seemed, to Thoreau, to be of some holy, higher realm, the depth of which few but himself might understand because it takes a higher view to understand it. Yet upon close examination, down close to the earth itself, Thoreau witnessed a battle between two classes of ants, black and red.[12] In them he saw men clashing, fighting, and the more he thought of it, "the less he saw the difference."[13] So here within his revered nature, when scrutinized deeply enough, Thoreau finds something wholly reminiscent of man and his lower nature. Thoreau is deeply excited, having "no doubt that it was a principle they fought for," and sees this wonderful battle in a mythological, heroic way.[14] But the truth is, he has no way of knowing whether this might be nature's counterpart to the American's war with Mexico, one class overrunning another for the basic desire to gain that which the other has. Thoreau writes that upon close examination Walden Pond is yellow in some places, green in others and, when viewed from some great height, appears to be blue, insinuating that the closer one scrutinizes a thing the more earthy it appears and

---

[12]Thoreau, 274-75.
[13]Ibid., 275.
[14]Ibid., 275-76.

This paper represents no slavish recital of Thoreau's principal beliefs. Instead, Bill *reports* the basic facts, *interprets* the words of Thoreau, and then *evaluates* the ideas in order to arrive, eventually, at his own critical perspective.

the higher one's point of view the more heavenly or spiritual a thing becomes.[15] Thoreau needed to realize how closely he scrutinized the government, its mass of men and the individual, and at what high and lofty heights he viewed nature and his own abilities. Then he might have realized that the evil did not lie in the government nor in humans as such; it resided in his point of view.

[15]Ibid., 235-36.

Works Cited

Lord Byron, George Gordon. "Sonnet on Chillon." <u>The
Mentor Book of Major British Poets</u>. Ed. Oscar
Williams. New York: Penguin, 1963.

Thoreau, Henry David. <u>Walden and Other Writings by
Henry David Thoreau</u>. New York: Bantam, 1989.

Wordsworth, William. "The World Is Too Much with
Us." <u>The Mentor Book of Major British Poets</u>. Ed.
Oscar Williams. New York: Penguin, 1963.

The Works
Cited
appears on a
separate
page.

Index